Victorian Rossendale

Lancashire's Rossendale Valley lies between Bury to the south and Burnley to the north and comprises several Victorian mill towns, the largest of which is Rawtenstall. The terrain is rugged moorland separating long, deep valleys, with the population concentrated along the valley bottoms. Its beauty is not that of the Yorkshire Dales or Cotswolds. Indeed, some might describe it as bleak, with abandoned stone quarries, boggy moorlands and reminders everywhere of our industrial past. However, Rossendale has its own beauty .... big hills sculptured by men's graft, bigger skies, hidden cloughs (small side valleys) and evidence all-around of the people who made it what it is today. We have woodlands, waterfalls, a gorge, remarkable views, fascinating museums, a steam heritage railway and friendly folk who, in exchange for a smile, are happy to chat and point you in the right direction.

Visitors and locals who escape to the hills are pleasantly surprised by what is considered, by many, to be Lancashire's 'hidden gem' and can be found roaming our footpaths, tracks and lanes.

In 1888, Marshall Mather was similarly impressed and published a book of walks called 'Rambles Round Rossendale', a compilation of articles he had written for the Rossendale Free Press, which is still our local newspaper.

Born in 1851, James Marshall Mather was a Methodist Minister in Rawtenstall and Manchester; an acclaimed author (whose works included two books on John Ruskin); historian; philosopher and would-be environmentalist. He wrote as J. Marshall Mather but was known to his family and friends simply as Marshall. Those who knew him said that he was an inspirational writer and preacher and combined a formidable intellect with humility and empathy with people from all walks of life. His personality shines through his books and he was, undoubtedly, an open-minded, compassionate, engaging and very likeable human being. At the age of forty-five, shortly after completing his second 'rambles' book, he became seriously ill, possibly with a degenerative disease, and was unable to walk or speak for the rest of his life. He died at the age of sixty-five in 1916.

Marshall's Rossendale was different from ours. To us, it is the area currently administered by Rossendale Borough Council, with clear, though arbitrary, boundaries. His was a much less rigidly defined area, known since ancient times as the Forest of Rossendale.

His style of writing is of its time, delightfully romantic and poetic and he uses far more adjectives than we now deem necessary. Unfortunately, he often fails to give clear route directions to his readers and instead, refers to local areas by names that would have been familiar to them and the occasional landmark, farm and ancestral hall. Following his rambles one hundred and thirty years later, using Victorian maps, can be frustrating but very satisfying when a piece of the jigsaw puzzle falls into place.

He comments on life in the mills; streams and rivers blackened by industrial waste; the inhabitants, good and bad, and the legends and history of the area. He regrets the passing of a perceived pre-industrial golden age which, at the time, was within the living memory of the oldest inhabitants and he preaches, as we might expect given his calling, the bounty of God and the impact of man's greed.

Marshall often hopped on and off the train at stations between Ramsbottom and Bacup (still possible by steam train on the East Lancs Railway between Ramsbottom and Rawtenstall) or simply walked from his home in Rawtenstall. He rambled at dawn and dusk, alone or with friends and, whatever the weather, time of day or season, he found beauty in his surroundings and sorrow in its despoliation by 'greedy' men.

Since the 1880s, housing developments have climbed the valleys' lower slopes but we can still walk on wild moorland, wander through mossy cloughs and admire distant views that Marshall would have known. Did he leave sufficient clues for us to follow his routes today? I decided to find out.

I have selected ten of Marshall's rambles (or parts thereof, where they are very long) and reproduced his original text where it relates to the route taken or the social history of the area. I have removed detailed family histories and much of his theological and philosophical commentary.

I describe how we can follow in his footsteps today. I have chosen to do so without the aid of maps or links to internet videos with, I hope you will agree, good reason. Like many walkers, I am often frustrated by guides which purport to be helpful, but aren't, because they contain inaccuracies or their routes have changed or been obstructed since they were written. My directions are based on public rights of way that can easily be followed today and, hopefully, will be for decades to come, without the need to read a map or look at a screen. Old-fashioned? Yes. Luddite? Possibly. A pleasant and practical way to follow a walk? Definitely!

Chapter headings and text in italics are Marshall's, the remainder are my own.

I hope you find this book interesting and enjoy exploring Marshall Mather's and my Rossendale Valley.

Andrew Gill

Some practical points about walking in Rossendale

It rains a lot here. The moors are often boggy, paths sometimes impassable and the ground underfoot can be very uneven with more trip hazards and slippery slopes than you can wave a stick at and, of course, we have hills …. lots of them. Depending on your level of fitness and ability, you might find the walks in this book physically challenging. Be prepared! Wear appropriate clothing and footwear, make sure someone knows where you're going and, ideally, have a mobile phone with you. Follow the Country Code and please leave my countryside as you find it.

In the more remote areas, especially on the moors, it is easy to lose your bearings and your way and you probably won't meet anyone to ask directions. My routes can be followed without a map and compass but, for your own safety, it is advisable to have them with you and know how to use them.

…. and about following my routes

These routes are for walking, not cycling, motorcycling or driving. I have chosen starting points where you can park nearby or access them by bus or train. The footpaths in my directions are just that and the lanes are either farm tracks or driveways to private homes, there is nowhere to park or turn-round and the owners are not going to thank you for trying!

Some of the paths and tracks that Marshall used are public rights of way but are currently difficult to access, as they are obstructed by foliage and fences. Where this is the case, I've chosen alternatives.

I ignore turnings that aren't on the route, so if my directions say go straight on and you find there are paths or lanes to the left or right, feel free to explore them (I can't resist them) but they are not part of the route. I sometimes use clock-face directions: 12 o'clock means straight on; 1 o'clock, bear right; 3 o'clock, turn right etc. All distances are approximate.

I only mention individual stiles and gates when I think it will help you find your way. Many stiles are being replaced by metal 'kissing' gates, so a walk description might be inaccurate in this respect.

If you intend to use buses or trains, check timetables as some services are infrequent and others seasonal. When parking on-street, please do so safely and legally.

My directions have been independently checked and are, I believe, correct at the date of publication. However, to err is human and if you spot a mistake, please let me know (contact details on the last page). If you find a route that has been obscured, obstructed or diverted, please report it to Lancashire County Council via their website. It's quick and easy to do and they can take appropriate steps to rectify the problem. By doing so, together we will ensure that our rights of way are protected for future generations.

.... and my definitions

Footpath - footpath; **Track** - wider than a footpath, can be vehicle-width; **Lane** - wider and with a better surface than a track; **Clough** - small valley, usually containing a stream; **Gulley** - shallow, valley-shaped depression which might or might not have a stream in it; **Lodge** - a large pond originally used to store water for a mill.

Finally, the disclaimer: you follow my routes at your own risk.

Index of walks

1. Stubbins to Irwell Vale - 4 miles: page 16

2. Cloughfold to Stacksteads - 2.5 miles: page 22

3. Bacup to Deerplay - 5.5 miles: page 27

3A. Bacup to the Irwell Spring - 6.5 miles: page 32

3B. Bacup to Thieveley Pike - 7 miles: page 33

4. Bacup to Broadclough Dykes - 2.5 miles: page 38

5. Rawtenstall to Chapel Hill - 1.3 miles: page 42

6. Rawtenstall to Cribden End via Crawshawbooth - 4 miles: page 48

7. Rawtenstall to Waugh's Well - 8 miles: page 59

8. Snig Hole Park to Musbury Tor - 2 miles: page 68

9. Snig Hole Park to Irwell Vale through Ravenshore Gorge - 2 miles: page 75

10. Haslingden Cemetery to Grane Head - 5 miles: page 85

Let's go walking ......

We'll set the scene with Marshall's opening chapter, which I have heavily edited. It is entitled 'Our Valley' and he surveys the area from Higher Meadow Head and Saunder Heights. These are the hills behind Marl Pits Leisure Centre, which is on the left as you go up Newchurch Road from Rawtenstall town centre.

Our Valley

Marshall says: *"The irregular ridges of hills that shut in the busy industries and shelter the meadow slopes of Rossendale are a minor spur of the great Pennine Range, commonly called the backbone of England. Through this valley flows the Irwell, with its tributaries, the Whitewell and the Limy, the three streams having their respective sources in high lands to the north-*

east. The area of the entire district is 300 square miles; its extreme boundaries touching the townships of Bury, Burnley, Todmorden and Rochdale.

To take in a full view of this mountain and moorland tract, we must see it from one of the many points of prospect afforded by the surrounding hills, than which none offers a better vantage than the Higher Meadow Head. From this outlook we see, sweeping up and stretching out, the three great ranges of the district. Of these, Cribden is by far the most imposing, its long line of crest rising in slow and stately gradient to a height of 1,300 feet above sea-level, and then falling in a succession of steps, towards the bottom lands of Flaxmoss and Cockham. The range that lies to our left, and forming the south-west boundary of the valley, runs up from Shuttleworth, and is of far more irregular outline, summit rising above summit, and slope intersecting slope, until their varied contours and uneven tops perplex the eye.

Stern Scout, with quarried breast and cloud-capped brow, recedes towards Fo' Edge; and the billowy stretches of Dearden Moor, with the rugged ridges of the far-famed Horncliffe Delfs, stand out like a bold promontory ere precipitately falling towards Balladen and Wood Top. Thence the ridge moves on towards Bacup, enclosing in its boundaries the Hall Carr Meadows and Whinberry Naze, which, together, bear upon their shoulders the oval form of Cowpe. Following these are Lenches, where patches of old forest, groups of huge boulders, intersections of winding paths and lone outlying folds, lie scattered in a rich picturesque.

Beyond, sweeps back the great land-bay of Cowpe; and also Brandwood, where dwelt the monks to whom first fell the thankless task of cultivating the wastes of Rossendale. Once more facing the south-west, we see between and beyond the end of Cribden and the slope of Dearden Moor a dim horizon of hills, which limits and encloses this portion of the valley.

In the nearer distance, and a mile and a half below where we stand, is the town of Rawtenstall, its crowded centre and outlying streets, in galleried heights and gradients, telling a tale of industry and growth. To the right nestles the hamlet of Crawshaw Booth, the Eden of the valley; while away to the left is the old fold in the Dead Queen's Clough, with its white-walled, scattered homes. A little below Seat Naze, the tower of Newchurch stands among a medley of surrounding roofs, the centre of ecclesiasticism, the home of culture, and the antiquaries' delight.

Upon a second glance, we find that all these scattered centres of population, though lying far apart, are linked together by continuous lines of dwellings, broken only by the many-storeyed factory and the towering chimney-top. Leaving Higher Meadow Head and climbing Saunder Heights, we secure a view of the valley Bacup-wards. Cliviger, Heald, Tooter Hill, Lowe Hill, and Brandwood lift themselves like giant watchers; while within and beneath their shadow lie the Tunstead Tops, the wilds of Wolfenden, the farmsteads of the Nab, and the slopes of Water. Here billowy stretches of heath and pasturage, patches of woodland and clough, banks of pit and quarry, ruins of silent mill and disused dwelling, gleams of reservoir and brooklet, though widely scattered, are all woven into a pattern of wild loveliness.

In the distance lies Bacup, from the north-east of which the road runs towards Burnley, that to the south-east leading to Facit and Rochdale. Should the traveller, however, refuse these turn-pike outlets and care to scale the heights beyond, he will find himself on the moorlands of Yorkshire, Todmorden, Heptonstall and Hebden Bridge, all lying within easy reach to the swift of foot. Thus our valley, though wild and bleak, possesses a boldness and grandeur of no mean character and even its climate, proverbial as it is for mist and rain, shares, in summer hours, a light and loveliness of which its occasional visitants and many detractors little dream.

Rossendale claims contiguity to Watling Street, from which the tread of the imperial troops resounded in echoes among the hills; and it also embraces within its limits the Broad Clough Dykes, of uncertain date and history. Though shorn of national historic glory, it is rich in local incident; for wherever man is, there is the story of a noble life.

From distant times to the present, Rossendale has enjoyed a gradual development of social and commercial life. Forestry gave place to grazing and agriculture and these, in their turn, were well-nigh superseded by manufacture. On the hill sides the sharp ring of the delf-man's pick is heard, in place of the woodman's axe and huntsman's horn and in the valley the spoom of spindles and the rattle of shuttles have for ever dissipated the reign of cold, continual peace.

The character of the Rossendale people is as marked as the natural features of the valley. Pronounced, individual, blunt, when once known they are never forgotten, and recognisable the wide world over. Their dialect is peculiarly their own and they possess a two-edged wit, which is too often mercilessly used. They love like angels, and they hate like devils: true as steel in their friendship, they never forgive or forget a foe. They are thrifty, but not mean; open-hearted, yet suspicious towards foreigners; independent, at times almost to stupidity. A sharp line of distinction is drawn between employers and employed and yet, withal, there is a freedom between these classes which, to a stranger, savours of "hail fellow, well met."

The mill-owners are large-hearted and lavishly generous, and their rapidly-earned wealth has been distributed with an unsurpassed munificence; yet they are not free from the idiosyncrasies peculiar to the sudden accumulation of great fortunes. The factory folk are bright, intelligent, well read in the best literature and keen as well as bitter in political ideas and strife. The inhabitants, if they only knew it, are among the highly-favoured of the earth. They have good wages; snug homes; a romantic district; libraries, newsrooms, and science classes, second only to those of our larger towns; and while within an easy range of the great centres of population, yet free from their smoke, and crowd, and sin."

Our River

Marshall follows the River Irwell from Stubbins near Ramsbottom to its source in the hills between Bacup and Burnley. We'll use his text for three very different walks; Stubbins to Irwell Vale, Cloughfold to Stacksteads and Bacup to Thieveley Pike. His preamble paints a dismal picture.

Marshall says: *"Here is a stream which for untold generations has been true to the law of its nature,* *save where thwarted and twisted and fouled by the hands of man. In times gone by, upon its banks, wild deer paused and started amid the forest glades, stealing down to cool their thirst. Within the falls and shallows once glanced and disappeared the leaping trout; while swift-winged birds, with sudden sweep, dipped their feathered breasts in the translucent wave.*

But suddenly, as in a dream when one awaketh, I turn from these fancies of a distant past to the realities before me. A disforested and disenchanted valley; a fouled and pestiferous stream, churned into filthy foam and discoloured with the refuse of a hundred mills; banks, bedraggled with the wrecks of rotting trunks; and thorn and briar-bush dotted with waste of cotton and webbed with threads of weft. Smooth stones, once the glory of the river's boulder bed, all stained with flow of blackened waters; and bobbins, corks, fragments of broken skips, and the decaying carcases of domestic animals, chasing one another, as in a dance of death, amongst the swirls and eddies. Thus before me runs the once beautiful river, now an open sink of feculent deposit, a miasma of death, a blackened and despoiling stream."

Stubbins to Irwell Vale

Marshall says: *"Though this is no highly-coloured picture of the Irwell as it flows through Rossendale, there are beauty spots upon its banks that well repay a visit. One such we find at Stubbin's Vale where we will join the river and ramble upwards towards its source. Passing beneath the railway arches, we follow the river to Chatterton Fold. Here stand the ruins of the mill around which waxed the famous fight in 1826, when Rossendale pitched her sons against the power of steam. Leaving the mill, we walk under the overhanging rocks, all moist with oozing waters and lush moss, and chasm'd with tiny rifts and clefts, towards Chatterton Wood, where the remains of forest glades and slopes of pasturage, rich with wild flowers, run out towards the river's bank. Now the Irwell takes a mighty sweep, which we follow and come to Alder Bottom and Green Hey Clough. Thence our path is parallel with the line to Lumb, where for a moment we must pause upon the bridge beneath the over-arching trees, looking through glades of foliage to where the*

river flows with sudden turn beneath a span of viaduct; and where, after seasons of flood, weed-fringed shallows mirror in their stillness the leaf and cloud forms of trees and sky. Our course now lies through Irwell Vale, a quiet pasturage of loveliness, towards which the brawling Ogden pours its waters, and where the gloomy gorge of Ravenshore dies away in wooded slope and fertile field."

Can we follow his route? Yes, in part, and we return by a parallel route that Marshall wouldn't have recommended to his readers, the railway line between Helmshore and Stubbins.

He refers to Chatterton Mill which was the scene of a Luddite revolt in 1826 when new technology was replacing traditional hand-loom weaving jobs. In the riot, six men were shot and died and many more were injured. Sixty-nine people were arrested and tried and either jailed or transported to Australia.

Walk 1: Circular walk from Stubbins to Irwell Vale

Distance: 4 miles

Features: quiet villages, a Victorian railway station and an impressive viaduct.

Terrain: mostly flat with one short, quite steep gradient; stiles and gates; some very uneven ground; some sections can be very muddy.

Starting point: Stubbins Street (near the junction of Bolton Road North and Stubbins Lane), Stubbins. Near-ish postcode BL0 0NJ.

Parking / Public transport: park on Stubbins Street. Ramsbottom is about half a mile away and has regular bus services and an East Lancs Railway Station.

Route: From Stubbins Street, at the traffic lights, turn left under the railway bridge and walk along Bolton Road North with the industrial estate on your right. Cross the river bridge and turn left into Chatterton Road. Pass Chatterton Mill on your left and continue through the village until you reach St Philip's Church on the left. Go straight ahead, down the lane, passing the playing fields and children's playground on the left (the scene of the Chatterton Mill Riots) until you reach the river. Take the path to the right, keeping the river on your left.

Follow this path and, at the corner of a field, turn left to cross a small footbridge. Continue on the path and a wall soon appears on the left. The East Lancs Railway is on the other side. Continue, for quarter of a mile, keeping the wall on your left, until the path dips to the left and walk under the railway line through a pedestrian tunnel. Now turn right onto a wider path with the river on your left and, when you reach the road, go straight ahead, with houses on your right and the river on your left. The photograph on the back cover was taken from the bridge to your left.

Just before the mini-mini-roundabout (yes, it's that small), turn right to visit Irwell Vale Railway Station. If the steam trains are running, it's a very special place to see one, if not, it's delightful anyway!

Retrace your steps to the mini-roundabout then cross the white-painted bridge over the River Irwell. After 50 yards, turn left into Bowker Street. At the end of the street, at the entrance to the Church, turn right into Milne Street, which soon becomes a rough track and climbs out of the village. At the top, where the path bends to the left and continues over a bridge, turn left **before** the bridge and take the slope down to the old railway track.

Continue for about a mile, including a section over a railway viaduct, until you reach the end of the tarmac track. Turn left onto a lane, then immediately left under the bridge into

Strongstry village. Go under the next railway bridge and take the well-signed footpath to the right, before the first house. Follow this path, with the river on your left, then turn sharp right where it meets a housing estate. Go straight on, to a path with houses on your left and their gardens on your right. Pass through the pedestrian tunnel under the railway line (this is the former site of Stubbins Station which Marshall would have known well) and turn left onto the road. At the road junction, bear slight left and you're back at the start point.

Cloughfold to Stacksteads

Marshall now heads upstream towards Rawtenstall but has very little to say about the Irwell as it passes through Rossendale's industrial heartland. The river was so polluted that he certainly wouldn't have recommended it as a country walk and, as most of his readers were likely to have lived and worked in the valley bottom between Rawtenstall and Bacup, they were probably already very familiar with the river. However, Marshall points out one interesting feature in Waterfoot that is straight out of a Dickens' novel!

Marshall says: *"There is one other view along the banks well worthy of a passing note. It is near Waterfoot and may be seen as we approach that station by train from Manchester. It lies below the level of the line and consists of a block of irregularly-built, many-storeyed houses, abutting upon the river, and rising from the bed of rock. The tottering walls are broken with recesses and jutted with landings and* *flights of stone steps lead down from their doorways to the waters beneath. These waters, which were originally crossed by stepping-stones, are now spanned by planks, over which the occupants gain egress and ingress to their dwellings.*

From this point forward to Broad Clough, the less we see and the less we say of the stream the better. It is merely a sink for manufacture, an open sewer for the flow of obnoxious matter. Its bed has been filled in with ashes which manufacturers have been too selfish to cart away and the accumulated filth of the mill dams is flushed week by week into its waters. Local authorities, afraid of rates, shoot their drainage towards its convenient falls and slatternly housewives toss their filth from out their doors upon the already obnoxious stream. That the age in which science finds utility for well-nigh all things, and in which aestheticism boasts of having trained a people's eye to beauty, should countenance this, is indeed a parody and a disgrace.

Yet the river's recuperative power is great. Only a few years ago, during a Whit week of heavy rains, and when the mills were stopped, the stream regained a purity which surprised the oldest inhabitant. True, it was not replenished with the finny tribe but the waters were fresh and the bed could be seen beneath their transparent flow."

Marshall used the train to start and finish walks, visit friends and travel further afield. He would have known the line between Rawtenstall and Bacup well. Today, it is possible to walk much of the track-bed and, in doing so, follow the River Irwell which is never far away.

Our next walk is not so much about following in Marshall's footsteps, as seeing what he saw from the train. We walk parallel to the valley's busiest and most industrial road, along the backs of what would then have been mills and are now industrial units and warehouses. So no distant views, but two, long, Victorian railway tunnels which, unusually, we walk through.

Walk 2: Cloughfold to Stacksteads

Distance: 2.5 miles (one way only)

Features: two Victorian railway tunnels, some grot spots but surprisingly pretty in places, especially beyond the tunnels.

Terrain: mostly designated cycle track, properly surfaced for much of its length but with one section of 70 yards which is very uneven underfoot. There are some gentle gradients.

Starting point: junction of Hill End Lane, Peel Street and Bacup Road (A681), Cloughfold. Near-ish postcode BB4 7LJ.

Parking / Public transport: park on-street nearby. There is a regular bus service between Stacksteads and Cloughfold so you can walk in one direction and catch the bus back or walk back along the same route.

Route: At the starting point, there is a wide surfaced cycle track between the main road and the river. Follow it or use the footpath that is adjacent to the wall by the river. After 500 yards, at the lane (Highfield Road, not signed) with the 'owl wearing a top hat' sculpture on the right, cross the lane and continue.

In 200 yards, cross another road (Lench Road, not signed) to stay on the path. Soon, it bends to the right. Turn left in front of the small building (the ground is very uneven here), then cross the bridge over the river. Pass through the 'tunnel' that is part of a modern warehouse. Go straight ahead to Bacup Road (A681) and turn right.

Cross the river, then take the road to the right, opposite the petrol station. After 100 yards, it bends to the left. Continue and, at the end, at the turning-circle with the mini-roundabout, take the path to the left, which becomes a back lane. This the location of Marshall's *"worthy of a passing note"* houses.

Go straight on until you reach Cowpe Road with the Health Centre to the right. Turn left over the bridge, then immediately right onto the cobbled path. The coal yard on the left is the former site of Waterfoot Railway Station.

Soon you'll see the first horseshoe-shaped railway tunnel. Although illuminated, it is dark, gloomy, atmospheric …. kids love it or hate it! This is soon followed by another, even longer one. Follow the surfaced path and, after a third of a mile, go straight across another road, Rakehead Lane (not signed) into the trees.

Continue on the surfaced track for a quarter of a mile until, after a long uphill slope, it merges with Blackwood Road (not signed). Bear left onto the road and, where it bends to the left to cross the river, take the track straight on, so that the river is on your left. After a few yards, cross either of the two bridges and turn right to stay on the path, with the river on your right. At the junction of paths (with the sports ground in front and to your right), turn left and you soon reach the main road (A681) between Rawtenstall and Bacup. Here you can catch a bus back to the starting point or turn round and walk back.

The Source of the River Irwell

Marshall knows how important the River Irwell is to Lancashire's booming economy. He appreciates the jobs that it provides as it passes through Rossendale, then Manchester, powering mills and transporting their output to the world. He sets out on an expedition to find its source.

Marshall says: *"To see it (*the River Irwell*) in its glory we must climb towards the springs. It was one Easter Monday when I paid my first pilgrimage to this shrine of waters.*

Keeping the turnpike road as far as Doles, we turned off towards the Irwell Springs Mill, the first of a long train of manufactories that owe their existence and prosperity to the course and the force of the river. Here the pure waters are first caught for man's service and first polluted by his ingenuity and commercial enterprise. Here, within a quarter of a mile of their source, they are diverted and stored, then flooded forth in defiled rush. From this point, until swollen and blackened, they flow through Manchester to the Mersey beyond, they are the great arterial current of the industries of North-East Lancashire. Riven mightier in bulk, and broader in sweep, and longer in course, there are many but few that turn so many wheels or yield a livelihood to so many families of toiling artisans.

We turned away from the Mill and pushed towards the Springs, walking by the bed of the stream and made towards the heights from which they start. We were soon lost amid a maze of troughs and well-nigh failed to find the source; but by dint of perseverance and careful selection, we followed, as we thought, the main artery, and at last, a little below the old Sandstone Quarry, found what we believed to be the river's pulse.

We climbed the hills beyond. To the right stood Thievely Pike, the beacon grounds where leaped the tongues of flame when watchers on the distant hill of Pendle were anxious for the signal news. To the West was Deerplay, one of the summits of the range of Cliviger. From this point one of the finest views of the surrounding country is gained. "From Thieveley Pike," says Whitaker, "where are the remains of an ancient beacon, is a very noble and diversified prospect, comprehending to the north almost the whole expanse of Craven, with the rocks of Settle, Malham, and Gordale, both Whernesides and Ingleboro, Penygent, Cam, and Graygreth Fell, north of Kirby Lonsdale; to the west and north-west Bowland, with its range of fells from Cross of Greet to Parlike, Longridge, part of Filde, with the western sea and in a sunny evening, when the tide is in, a noble expanse of the estuary of the Ribble, like a sheet of gold. More to the south the prospect is circumscribed by Cribden and other high grounds betwixt us and the great plain of Lancashire but these are seen occasionally, though rarely, surmounted by three conical summits of the

Carnarvonshire hills, one of which, from its form and elevation, I suspect to be Carnedd Llewellyn. Directly south-ward a single opening exhibits the town of Manchester, enveloped in eternal smoke, with the high grounds near Dishley and the Park of Lyme, in Cheshire; while beyond, and south-eastward, further prospect is barred by the long and lofty ridges of the Peakish hills. The northern and southern extremities of this great map are at least 120 miles distant from each another."

Can we follow his route? Yes but he sometimes walks along the stream-bed and this isn't possible or practical today. So, we head in the same direction as Marshall and follow the Irwell as river, then stream, as best we can. What we now know to be its source might not be the one that he found. Thieveley Pike won't have changed but whereas he stood on the summit, we have to be satisfied with standing six feet away, as the trig point is on the other side of a fence.

Walk 3 has two optional extensions, 3A and 3B so you can decide how adventurous you want to be. Walk 3 is a rural meander, following the River Irwell until it's just a babbling brook. 3A visits the River's source and 3B climbs to Thieveley Pike.

Walk 3: Circular walk from Bacup to Deerplay

Distance: 5.5 miles

Features: quiet back lanes, a rural delight.

Terrain: some not-too-steep gradients; stiles and gates; some very uneven ground; sometimes very muddy.

Starting point: Bacup town centre. Near-ish postcode OL13 9NH.

Parking / Public transport: park on-street nearby. Bacup has regular bus services.

Route: From the fountain in the centre of Bacup, walk north along Burnley Road for a few yards, then right into Boston Road. The photograph below, of this location, was taken in the 1890s.

At the end of Boston Road, turn left up Lane Head Lane. At the Cricket Ground wall, bear left onto Blackthorn Lane, then next right onto Cowtoot Lane.

Pass the football club on the left and the school on the right and continue up the track passing 'West View' terrace on the left. Pass through a gate and onto a footpath which climbs up the hill with houses on the right and a field on the left. Turn left after the large cone-shaped sculpture, keeping the wall and fence posts on your right.

Look across the valley from here for a good view of Broadclough Dykes (see Walk 4).

Soon the path is enclosed by walls on each side and then drops to the left and is 'sunken'. Pass under the stone arch (the photo was taken in the opposite direction).

Soon, at a farm, the path becomes a track, 'Old Meadows Road' (not signed). Follow it through another farm, then a right / left 'S' bend, then another farm. A little further on, at a small group of buildings where the lane bends sharply to the left, go straight on keeping the bungalow on your left. Follow the lane in front of a house and then around the end of it and, at the 'V' junction of two tracks, take the left one.

After 200 yards a farm lane joins from the left. In another 100 yards, the lane divides in front of a large modern-ish barn (hidden behind some trees). Take the left fork, keeping the barn on your right. This becomes a path which bends to the left and crosses a stream. Continue with trees on your left and fields on your right. After another 100 yards, take the path to the right in a 2 o'clock direction. The River Irwell is now on your left and a pedestrian bridge soon comes into view. Cross the bridge and turn right on the other side. When you reach the road, turn right up Beaufort Road with houses on your left and trees (and the Irwell therein) on your right. At the junction at the top of the road, turn left. At the end of the road, at a T junction, turn right into Heald Lane.

The lane becomes a track with a stream (the Irwell) to the right. Follow it, pass a pylon on your left with a lodge (large pond) in front of you. The track bends to the left and uphill. At the cluster of buildings at the top (Heald Lane Farm), take the footpath immediately to the left of the house in front of you. Follow this path (notice the Church Memorial on your right) and, at the end, turn left down the tarmac lane. There is a RW (Rossendale Way) circular sign here.

Go down the lane and follow it round to the right, over a stream (yes, it's the Irwell), then another bend to the right. After a few yards, as the lane widens out and bends sharply to the left, you'll see a stile and a footpath going up a grassy bank in front of you. Follow this grass path up the hill and over a field stile and aim to the left of the small square building on the skyline. At the top, use the stone 'steps' in the wall to climb over it and walk a few yards to the main road (Burnley Road).

(This is the starting point for Walk 3A if you intend to walk to the Irwell Spring or Thieveley Pike. If not, continue below.)

Turn right onto the main road and walk up the hill and round to the left for a third of a mile, then turn sharp left onto Bacup Old Road. Stay on this road (which becomes a track) for one and a half miles eventually reaching Burnley Road (A671). Turn right and walk down Burnley Road with the River Irwell running alongside on your left.

In 250 yards you pass, on the right, the farm lane that takes you to Broadclough Dykes (Walk 4) so you can divert here to see them or continue down the main road to your starting point, Bacup town centre.

Walk 3A: Bacup to the River Irwell

Distance: 6.5 miles for the Bacup to Irwell Spring circular walk

Features: a mine water treatment plant!

Terrain: some not-too-steep gradients; mostly paths but the last one hundred yards is across rough moorland and can be boggy and inaccessible.

Starting point: as described above in Walk 3.

Route: Having climbed over the wall, instead of joining the main road turn immediately right over the stile next to the full-width gate and, after a few yards, bear left so that the small brick building is on your left. The track drops into a shallow gulley. Follow it down and then up towards the solar panels. (Interestingly, this processing plant is owned by the Coal Authority and is cleaning water from coal mines that closed decades ago.)

Pass to the left of the solar panels and, at the fence in front of you, turn left. After a few yards, turn right, keeping the same fence on your right and head for the tall, wooden, electrical pole next to a fenced compound. Cross the stile to the right of the gate and, after about 20 yards, turn left onto the moor. There's no path, so walk parallel to the fence on your left and, after about 100 yards, you'll see a shallow depression and a spring. You've reached the Irwell Spring, the source of the River Irwell.

Retrace your steps across the moor to the track. You now have a choice. You can turn right to return to the starting point of Walk 3A, then follow the remainder of Walk 3 or turn left, to continue to Thieveley Pike on Walk 3B.

Walk 3B: Bacup to Thieveley Pike

Distance: 7 miles for the Bacup to Thieveley Pike circular walk

Features: amazing views from Thieveley Pike and, on the way back, of the valley between Weir and Bacup.

Terrain: We cross wild moorland which is unforgiving territory …. rough underfoot, boggy, remote, pathless in places. **Only attempt this walk if you have appropriate clothing, equipment and bog-hopping experience.**

Starting point: The track 100 yards from Irwell Spring.

Route: Having turned left from the moor onto the track, walk towards the fenced compound. When you reach it, turn right and then left around its side, then climb the hill on the muddy track. The path is obvious for a few yards but then disappears. Head up the hill in same direction and, after 200 yards, it becomes a wide, grass track. Continue up the hill with the Thieveley Pike trig point on the skyline in the 1 o'clock direction. Make your way to the trig point, which is behind a fence, and admire the view.

With your back to the trig point, turn right onto the track, keeping the wall and fence on your right. After 250 yards, another wall (or what's left of it) appears on the left, at right angles to your direction of travel. Turn left immediately after it, so that the wall is now on your left. The path is very indistinct but proceed keeping the wall on your left.

The wall ends as you start to climb over a low grassy mound. Keep heading in the same direction and pass to the left of a tall wooden post. The wall starts again, keep it on your left. When it ends again, pass over another, higher and longer, grassy mound and descend to a stile. Go over the stile and descend, keeping a wall and fence on your right. Enter a narrower section, fenced on both sides. At the end, turn right over a stile, then immediately left over another. Cross two more stiles to join the main road.

At the road, turn left and then right onto Bacup Old Road. Stay on this road (which becomes a track) for one and a half miles eventually reaching Burnley Road (A671). Turn right and walk down Burnley Road with the River Irwell running alongside on your left.

In 250 yards you pass, on the right, the farm lane that takes you to Broadclough Dykes (Walk 4) so you can divert here to see them or continue down the main road to your starting point, Bacup town centre.

Broadclough Dykes

A short walk to see the 'Dykes', Rossendale's mysterious ancient earthwork.

Marshall says: *We stopped to look at Broad Clough Hall, dating back to the year 1666. It is an ideal home, standing amongst the many-coloured foliage of ancestral trees and sheltered by surrounding knolls. A little higher up the road we came to the gigantic excavations known as the 'Dykes.' Eighteen hundred feet in length and over fifty feet in width, they remain without date or veritable tradition. The Historian of Whalley supposes them to be the remains of a vast British camp but Mr. Newbigging argues, with great weight of evidence, that they constituted a portion of the line of defence raised at the time of the great strife between the Saxons and the Danes, near Burnley.*

Can we follow his route? Although we don't know which lanes or footpaths Marshall used to reach the Dykes, the most likely one, that is still a right of way, is at the time of writing, blocked by foliage and fences.

Until these issues are resolved, we will take a less-direct but easy-to-follow route. Unfortunately, most of it is along a busy main road.

We will pass Broad Clough Hall but cannot see it from this route. As for Broadclough Dykes, we know no more about their age or purpose now than Marshall did one hundred and thirty years ago. There was a limited archaeological dig in the 1970s but it proved inconclusive.

When you arrive at the Dykes, you might be disappointed. They comprise a long mound of earth behind which is a trench and line of trees, pleasant enough but not spectacular and it is private land. A public right of way runs parallel to the Dykes, a little further down the hill, but you can't get a good view of them from the path. They are more distinct and impressive from the other side of the valley (on Walk 3). Look for a wide, narrow field below a line of trees, which is noticeably smoother than those around it.

…… and the answer to the question 'can we follow his route?' is 'no'.

Walk 4: Bacup to the Broadclough Dykes

Distance: 2.5 miles (whole walk)

Features: an ancient earthwork

Terrain: a gentle climb from Bacup which gets much steeper as we approach the Dykes; gates and a stile; generally good paths and tracks.

Starting point: Bacup town centre. Near-ish postcode OL13 9NH.

Parking / Public transport: park on-street nearby. Bacup has regular bus services.

Route: From the fountain in the centre of Bacup, take Burnley Road for just under a mile. Pass a small 'Coal Authority' building on the right, then old mill buildings on the left and turn left between the end of the mill and the semi-detached houses (Broadclough Villas) onto the farm track signed 'Dykes House Farm Private Road'.

At the top of the long, straight, steep track, cross the stile to the right of the house and the Dykes are on the hillside to your left. Return to Bacup by the same route in reverse.

The Graveyard among the Mountains

Marshall says: *"It was here, at Chapel Hill, upon the lone mountain side, within an enclosure of walls all lichen-grown and grey, roofed in by clouds and paved by the long, dank grass, that the Society of Friends sought shelter from the persecutions of men for their silent adorations, as well as a resting place for their beloved dead.*

Chapel Hill is rightly named, its ecclesiastical associations reaching back to anti-reformation times. It was originally a retreat for a brotherhood of Roman Catholic recluses, who built and inhabited the old farmstead now adjoining the burial ground, and the remains of a piscina, recessed within the crumbling walls a little above the porch, are still to be seen. It is generally supposed that the name 'Chapel Hill' was derived from its associations with the Friends' Meeting House but this is not so, for amongst the earliest recorded births are those of the younger children of James and Alice Radcliff, of 'Chapel Hill'. This at once proves the name as associated with the farmstead prior to the advent of Quakerism and, what is more, no Quaker would call any place for worship by other name than 'Meeting House.'

Members of this sect became the subjects of cruel persecution, the chief cause being their refusal to pay tithes. Magistrates showed little mercy to these conscientious men, when arraigned by the informers before the tribunal. Many from Rossendale were confined amongst the lowest class of criminals, and exposed to raging disease, in the Castle of Lancaster. Their bodies were brought home in the July and August of 1692 and laid to rest in the burial ground at Chapel Hill.

The Chapel Hill Burial Ground is an enclosure measuring some fifteen yards by twelve and fronts the narrow winding path once serving as highway between Rawtenstall and Lumb. Over the entrance is an inscription stone, bearing the original date of opening as 1663, as also the date of its re-erection, 1847. Leading from the entrance is a central path, or aisle, at the further end of which lies a slab of stone, whereon stood the men and women of this silent sect when moved to utterance by the inbreathing spirit. Up to within the last few years, stone seats projected from the walls by way of rest for the members of the congregation after their weary marches and stormy journeys to this their place of prayer, but unfortunately these have been destroyed by vandal hands. Around, and unmarked by mound or slab, are the underlying dead, while above, tall grasses sigh to the moorland breeze, and trees, like funeral plumes, wave in shadow.

One hundred and thirty-five souls have found Christian interment and though none can re-count the record of their lives, or gauge the influence started and still streaming, from their simple character and unknown labour, yet none will deny that they, though dead, yet speak.

The question still remains, why, if Meeting House as well as burial-ground, the enclosure was left unroofed? There is a tradition, still cherished by the Friends, that the walls were uncovered in order that the sect might escape the rigorous laws of the Conventicle Act, for it punished with fine, imprisonment, and transportation on a third offence, all persons who met in greater number than five for any religious worship save that of Common Prayer. In 1715, land was secured at Crawshaw Booth upon which the present Meeting House was erected, at a cost of £69, towards which Rossendale contributed £30. It was opened in the May of 1716 and from that time to the present, the meetings have been held in unbroken succession.

It is worthy of note that on the 22nd of February, 1818, the illustrious Elizabeth Fry was amongst the members who worshipped there and the books contain records of many other equally noted members of the Society as being in attendance from time to time, some of whom were visitors from the States.

Spots such as these give sanctity to the valley. Long may they remain untouched and long may their associations and history give inspiration to those who dwell beneath their shadow."

Can we follow his route? Although we don't know which route Marshall took, ours uses lanes which he would have known, so the answer is probably 'yes'.

The Friends Meeting House in Crawshawbooth is still a Quaker place of worship. Less well-known is the Burial Ground on Chapel Hill. This too is used for service 'though only once a year.

Walk 5: Circular walk from Rawtenstall to Chapel Hill

Distance: 1.3 miles

Features: a three hundred and fifty year old Quaker Burial Ground and lovely views over the Rossendale Valley.

Terrain: uphill all the way (and downhill all the way back!), steep in places; some very rough ground; sometimes muddy.

Starting point: Rawtenstall Market, Newchurch Road, Rawtenstall. Near-ish postcode BB4 7QX.

Parking / Public transport: park in a town centre public car park (you'll need a parking disc obtainable from local shops) or on-street nearby. Rawtenstall Bus Station and the East Lancs Railway Station are less half a mile away.

Route: From the Market, go up Newchurch Road and take the second street on the left, Whitehead Street, and keep left of the church converted into flats. At the top, turn right onto Hurst Lane which flattens out, bends to the left and narrows. Continue up the hill and after 300 yards, at the a Y-shaped junction (with a salt bin), take the right fork. The first house on the right is Chapel Hill Farm and the Quaker Burial Ground is after and adjacent to it.

Continue up the lane bearing to the right and, at the next house on the right, turn right onto the track in front of it. The track bends to the right and then to the left and becomes a footpath. When you reach Waingate village, go straight on and, at the last house on the right, take the steeply descending footpath in front of you. Follow this, keeping the stream on your left, until you reach the main road. Turn right and walk down Newchurch Road to return to the starting point.

A ramble up the Rake in the gloaming

Marshall says: *"For some years I have been a wanderer, if not upon the face of the earth, at any rate upon that portion of its face known as Rossendale. Roaming the hill sides in search of wooded cloughs where shadows reign and waters pause and fall and footing the fields where wild flowers grow and wild birds warble, Rossendale has become a little world to me, a little world of never-wearying beauty and ever-suggestive change. No wonder, then, that I felt somewhat taken aback when a friend of mine led me by a way, the most delightful part of which I knew not, and I was all the richer for having another line of travel laid down upon the map of my peregrinations.*

Threading our way through the Fold, the High Street of ancient Rawtenstall, we traversed the banks of the blackened stream known as the Limy or Lurny. Who would think the present dilapidated and tortuous street, together with the befouled and partly tunnelled stream, once formed the beautiful Routand Clough? Here the waters came leaping and foaming down from the heights of Gambleside, roaring and swirling around and over the stepping-stones that spanned them at the Fold, the wooded slopes of Holly Mount falling almost perpendicularly from the level of the present observatory to their foot. Here came the Saxon hunters in search of sport, the noise of the river leading them to name the spot Routand, the brawling brook; from which some suppose the name of the present village, perverted from Routonstall to Rawtenstall, takes its origin.

From the Tup Bridge we followed the Burnley Road as far as the north-east boundary of the Cemetery and held our way beneath the shadow of its wall until the hoarding of the football field was gained. Here we turned off towards the Constable-lee meadows, pausing for a moment to glance up the Lee Clough, by no means one of the least attractive spots in the district and in which I have spent many a contemplative hour. Crossing what in rainy seasons is the fall of the stream which flows down this wooded glen, we continued our way towards the old hall at Constable-lee. It is, I believe, one of the earliest structures now standing in our district, and was once, in some way or other associated with the office of greave or constable of the forest.

A little higher up the Holly Lane stands another old Greave House bearing over its porch the initials A. L.

E. and the date 1708. The initials stood for Lawrence and Elizabeth Ashworth, the estate still being in the family. About fifty years ago it was thickly wooded, the then owner cutting down and clearing off the timber for £200, the timber being sold at 5d. per foot. The present occupier, who was then a mere lad, took this sacrifice of trees sadly to heart and at his own trouble and expense went far and wide for saplings and slips and himself replanted the estate. He said to me, the other day, "There's not a tree on this estate but I've carried it in my hands."

Crossing Holly Lane, we kept the field path to Higher Constable-lee and passing the Grange and the Higher Constable-lee Farm, followed Reed's Lane, keeping Reed's Farm on our left. The fields now entered presented a vantage ground from which a fine view of the valley was gained. To the left stood Crawshaw Hall, boldly prominent from amid its background of wooded slopes, the moorlands of the Cribden range rising behind; while to the right ran the long and uneven line of hill, studded with farm-steads which separates the Crawshawbooth Valley from the valley of Water beyond. Before us was the village of Goodshaw with its chapel and here and there tall chimneys that told of manufacture's mighty power. The fields through which we passed were rich in their growth of wild flowers.

Reaching the end of the field path we turned towards Rushbed. We soon found ourselves passing through a farmyard, finally emerging upon the bridge spanning the river near the printworks. A few steps brought us to the road which skirts the grounds of Crawshaw Hall and passes its entrance gates. Through the entrance gates we get a glimpse of the fine facade of Crawshall Hall, sheltered amid its acres of wooded slope. Crossing the turnpike, we took a sudden turn up the opening between the Crawshaw Hall and Sunnyside estates, passing under a lengthy archway by which they are connected. Thence, opened out before us a steep and tortuous path, rocky-bottomed and fenced in by rude stone walls. Overhanging these were the interlacing branches of ash and sycamore, beech and birch. Arriving at the outlet, we crossed the fields to the Laund Farm. Bleak upon the mid-heights of Cribden, weather-stained with a hundred winters, the dwelling-place of generations of hardy tillers of the soil.

It was a wild evening, and the storm spirit was abroad on these tops. Lengthening shadows and falling damps quickened our somewhat flagging steps and we pushed towards Cribden End and rapidly rounded the Clough. In the gathering darkness it possessed a fascination of terror. The wind, moaning up its gorge, sweeping through the foliage of its trees, touching into plaintive music its rushes and long grasses, seemed as though it wanted to be disburdened of some woe. No wonder, thought I, our forefathers associated with such sights and sounds with the boggart and the wraith; no wonder that Lancashire tradition is so rich in its stories of the supernatural and the mysterious.

Once in the valley, we neared my friend's house, which, for a few hours, was to be my hospice. Here a kindly fire was kindled, and the remainder of the evening spent in quiet chat."

Can we follow his route? Yes, in part.

About half of the walk that Marshall describes has been obliterated by a dual-carriageway and residential development but that which remains has wonderful views. His starting point, 'The Fold', Rawtenstall's original main street, was where St. Mary's Way is now. There is, though, a nod to its existence as the small garden area between St. Mary's Church and the ASDA traffic lights is called 'Old Fold Garden' and is lovingly maintained by volunteers. Much of his route along the east side of Burnley Road is now a succession of housing estates but by climbing a little higher up the hill, we can walk parallel to his route and see what he saw. We then descend into Crawshawbooth and follow in Marshall's footsteps along the hills to the west of Burnley Road and back to Rawtenstall.

Walk 6: Circular walk from Rawtenstall to Cribden End via Crawshawbooth

Distance: 4 miles

Features: a disguised Victorian chimney; lovely views from the hills on each side of the Rawtenstall to Crawshawbooth valley.

Terrain: lots of hills, some long and steep; gates and stiles; very uneven underfoot in places; can be very muddy.

Starting point: Rawtenstall Market, Newchurch Road, Rawtenstall. Near-ish postcode BB4 7QX.

Parking / Public transport: park in a public car park (you'll need a parking disc obtainable from local shops) or on-street nearby. Rawtenstall Bus Station and the East Lancs Railway Station are less than half a mile away.

Route: From the Market, go up Newchurch Road and take the second street on the left, Whitehead Street, keeping left of the church converted into flats. At the top, turn right onto Hurst Lane. After it flattens out and bends to left, it narrows and continues up the hill. After 300 yards, where the lane divides at a Y-shaped junction (with a salt bin), take the left fork.

At the top of the lane, take the stepping-stone footpath across the lawn to the right of the house in front of you, go up the steps and turn right onto the footpath, then left onto a lane. After 70 yards, take the footpath through the trees on the left. Go over a stile then head diagonally right up the hill, aiming for the gap in the wall. Go through a gate, then the gap and, keeping a wall on your left, continue through two pedestrian gates, then two full-width gates next to a farmhouse on your left.

Continue along the track. If you look over to the opposite side of the valley, you can see Crawshaw Hall (referred to by Marshall) nestling in the wood in the 10 o'clock direction and the farms between the skyline and the treeline are on the return section of our walk.

Pass through a wooded area at Edge End Farm (the name plaque can be seen by looking back once you've passed it). After the next house on the left, the track descends and as it starts to bend to the right, go through the metal gate next to a full-width gate, on your left. Then walk diagonally left, down the field towards the wall.

Continue down the slope, keeping the wall on your left, then down the steps. At the bottom of the steps, go straight on and cross a road (Crawshaw Drive) onto an enclosed footpath. At the bottom of the footpath, turn right onto a road, Hollin Way, which then bends to the left and joins the main road from Rawtenstall to Crawshawbooth (A682).

Turn right onto the main road and, at the brow of the hill, on the left, you'll see the drive to Crawshaw Hall that Marshall so admired. Just 50 yards further on, on the same side of the road, there is footpath (called 'Hugh Rake' but not signed) immediately to the left of the gates and drive to a large house. Turn left onto this footpath. It is narrow, muddy, long and steep but worth the effort when you get to the top.

As you approach the top, look up to your right to see a large square building on the hill amongst the trees. Built in 1839, it was the chimney of an underground flue from the Sunnyside Printworks in Crawshawbooth.

The path broadens out and becomes a walled grass track that bends to the left, then takes a sharp right, up a hill towards a farm.

At the farm, go through the gate and turn diagonally left up the lane. At the next farm, the track stops but continues as a footpath to the right and at the back of the farmhouse. The footpath continues to climb and, after a gate, does so to the left of a shallow gulley. After another gate, it flattens out onto a broad grassy ledge.

As it descends, at a wooden signpost bear left down a narrower path towards a wood. Pass through the wood and where it meets the lane and farmhouse, bear diagonally left across the yard to join another footpath to the right of a small gate.

Follow this path, heading generally in the direction of a communications mast which soon comes into view, skirting a deep clough (that Marshall mentions), eventually becoming a broad, stone and grass track that leads to a gate. (There is a spring to your right with a stone in memory of 'Sue'.)

Go through the gate and turn sharp left. Follow this well-used stone footpath down the hill towards the communications mast and pass it on your left. Continue and, at the bottom of the path, turn right onto Beech Street, then right onto Greenfield Street and left into Whittle Street. At the bottom, turn sharp left to the traffic lights. The Market, your starting point, is just across the road on the left.

Waugh's Well

Marshall says: *"Edwin Waugh is the poet of Lancashire. What Scott did for his native wilds and Wordsworth for his much-loved mountains, Waugh has done for the scattered folds and moorland haunts of the County Palatine. He is the poet of the people, their toils, their sorrows, their mirthfulness and pastimes, their sufferings and their death. Why Lancashire is so quick to appreciate the works, and yet so slow to publicly recognise the genius of this, her greatest poet, I know not but I believe I am correct in stating that the only memorial raised to his life-long work in provincial literature is a rude stone structure marking a moorland spring upon the heights of Fo' Edge, in Rossendale.*

There are several paths by which this well is reached. The one I oftenest tread is by Lomas Lane and

Balladen Road. The road to Balladen runs off to the right and from this, the original route to Manchester, a fine view of the surrounding valley is gained. Here lie the scattered ruins of old mills, with an ancient dwelling at the foot of the clough, a clump of trees still flinging a welcome shade across its portals and over the stream as it winds its onward way. A few hundred yards further are the famous Horncliffe Delfs, from out of which some of our best English stone has been hewn. Those who know these delfs only from a distance know but little of the vast area of their excavations. They are now a vast field of well-nigh disused pits and heaps of shale and scaplings, a rocky wilderness, a desert of stone. Yet it is pleasing to note how nature is gradually shaping into symmetrical contour and carpeting with vegetation, their hard lines and barren surfaces.

From Balladen I follow the foot-road that ridges Hawke's Clough, once the pride of the valley and still a favourite resort for the naturalist and botanist and lovers of rural quiet. Within the last forty years the pink and white hawthorn flowered abundantly upon these hill-sides, together with the wild rose, the mountain ash, and dogberry. But now they are sought for in vain. And why? Smoke? Not smoke alone; but the depredations of a rising population that smoke has reared and more destructive far in their ravages than the vapour out of which they spring. The truth is these solitudes have been despoiled by gangs of youths whose only amusement is wilful sacrilege in the nature-temples of God. Broken branches, uprooted shrubs, choked streams and madly-trampled flower meads, this for years has been the pastime of the offspring of the valley; and to-day a torn and bleeding vegetation, a vegetation whose glory is fast departing, appeals in mute significance to those who still love the shadow of its remaining foliage and the beauty of its now sparsely scattered flowers.

This clough opens out upon Dearden Moor, then Sand Beds Lane which, beyond the Sand Beds Farm, is now impassable to all save those who are sure of foot. The cart ruts are worn away by the erasure of the mountain torrent and present the phenomenon of a clough in formation. Already the herbage of the moorland is creeping over the gapped and ruined wall on either side and spreading down the ever-deepening slope. When it is remembered that the cloughs of Rossendale are the workmanship of these ever-wearing streams, it needs no stretch of imagination to go back to when the deepest of them was as shallow as this already forming in Sand Beds Lane.

The lane leads to the foot of the hill known as Cowpe Lowe. From this point the traveller must keep the ridge towards Fo' Edge; not forgetting, however, to pass for a moment beneath the opening to the left and situate mid-way in the bend of the tram-line embankment. About a hundred yards below this opening is the surprise view of Rossendale.

I know of no spot in our district where the change of scene is so sudden and so complete; and many an old inhabitant is baffled when unexpectedly brought face to face with the extended view. This may be easily understood when it is remembered that the vantage ground is the dividing ridge between the Edenfield and Cowpe valleys; and so sharp is the bend round the foot of the Lowe, that it is possible to stand on Fo' Edge and watch the train leave Stubbins station and then walk down the declivity at the further side in time to catch the same at Waterfoot. Within a hundred yards, the spectator may take in the sweep of Bury, Holcombe, Musbury, and Haslingden and then look out upon New Church, Water, Booth Fold, and Stacksteads, and the distant ranges of Cliviger, and Heald Moor beyond.

To gain the well, I retrace my steps, and keep the tram tracks until reaching the three farmsteads of Pike Slack, Four Acre, and Fo' Edge. These three dwellings, almost equidistant, stand like sentinels a little below the quarried heights of the ridge and face the precipitate gorge which lies in gloom below. Rude stone structures these, weather-worn and time-stained, lichen-grown and hoary, yet eloquent with the stories of a moorland life. Many a time have I sought their friendly shelter, and many a time listened to the garrulous traditionary talk of the old occupant of Pike Slack. Far away from the pulsing tide of life, these simple moorland folk share one another's joys and sorrows, aspirations, and defeats; and their little world, though compassed by an acre of out-lying pasturage, is none the less a world to them.

About five hundred yards from the last-named farmstead, and lying right along the footpath, the traveller comes upon the well. It is an unpretentious structure, with wings and seats on either side; the water falling from out a spring into a central recess or trough. It was opened in the summer of 1866, dinner being sent up from the valley, and served by "Owd Ann," at Fo' Edge Farm; after which the company adjourned to the well, when it was christened with some little ceremony, many friendly speeches being made in the open air and from the breezy mountain top.

There are few grander views in Lancashire than that gained from the well. On the left, and rising to the height of fifteen hundred feet above sea level, frown the mountain solitudes of Scout. The counter-slope of the valley is less stern and lone, a few farmsteads studding its expanse, and pasturage enlivening its monotony; but the falls below are deep and dark, and from out their depths rise the sound of many waters. Well have the natives of these wilds termed them Hell Clough, for their fastnesses are ever clouded with shadow, while a heedless step might precipitate into fatal depths.

Again, the view from the well affords a grand outline of the surrounding hills. Beyond is the range of Holcombe and Musbury Tor, the valley of the Irwell running at their base and studded alike with its factories and its farms. Nearer, sweep the moors of Dearden, yielding to the Close of Newhall that swells in sea of grass far up the clough. To the right, the oval form of Cowpe lifts high its brow; while behind are the heights of Fo' Edge. Wherever the eye falls there is meadow and moorland, mountain solitude and lonesome gorge.

Often, as I leave this spot, my mind is burdened with thoughts too deep for utterance; and as often do I find a floodgate in some of those songs so sweetly sung by him to whose shrine my pilgrimage has been paid, and to whom I have breathed my best of wishes in draughts from the well that bears his name."

Can we follow his route? Yes, 'though we divert occasionally because of 'lost' footpaths.

The above is a much-shortened version of Marshall's ramble to Waugh's Well. I have visited it many times and, like Marshall, find that it's a great place to press my pause button and, with flask and butties, take in the remarkable view and contemplate the meaning of 'life, the universe and everything'. I recommend it.

Walk 7: Rawtenstall to Waugh's Well

Distance: 8 miles

Features: Fo' Edge Farm, Waugh's Well and glorious views.

Terrain: this is a four mile climb, sometimes steep; gates and stiles; very uneven underfoot in places, can be very boggy, sometimes impassable.

Starting point: The East Lancs Railway Station, Rawtenstall. Near-ish postcode BB4 6AG.

Parking / Public transport: park on-street nearby. Rawtenstall Bus Station is just a few minutes' walk away.

Route: From the Railway Station turn right onto Bury Road. Pass the row of shops on the left then turn left into Lomas Lane. Cross a junction and continue up Lomas Lane. Where it takes a sharp right turn, turn right. After half a mile, at the end of the lane, take the footpath that ascends into the wood in front of you. It divides but either path will soon bring you to a road. Turn left. The road bends round to the right then continues, flat and straight, towards a farm in the distance.

Enter the farmyard then turn right, keeping the farmhouse on your right, and exit the yard through the gate. Where the lane bends down to the right, take the narrow stone path in front of you. Pass an old quarry on your left, then a modern house above you on the left. This is Gincroft Lane but is not signed. Pass a wide metal gate (green at the time of writing) on your left and descend to the junction with Sand Beds Lane (not signed). Turn sharp left, up the hill, on a broad track.

After half a mile, pass a derelict farmhouse on your left then, in 50 yards, bear right into a field and take a grass path up the hill, keeping a deep gulley on your right. In the top right-hand corner of the field, go through a pedestrian gate and continue on the footpath. It broadens into a track and, at the foot of the hill (Cowpe Lowe), cross a deep, wide ditch with impressive stonework and turn right.

Follow the track keeping Cowpe Lowe on your left. If you look over to the right, you can see our destination, Waugh's Well, on the hillside to the left of the reservoir. Stay on the stone track (notice the cart ruts worn into the stone) keeping the wall on your right. Sometimes, this track is so boggy as to be impassable and you can follow its route, twenty or so yards to the left along the old tramway embankment.

When you reach the junction of paths (including the Pendle Bridleway) at a wooden signpost, turn sharp right onto the narrow grass path heading across the moor towards the windmills. Where it meets a track from the left, continue in the same direction keeping the wall on your right. Where it meets another track coming down the hill on your left and merges with a concrete one on the right, take the concrete track and continue towards the windmills.

Leave the concrete track where it bends right downhill and bear slight left onto a broad grass track. You soon reach the remains of Fo' Edge Farm, where an information board explains the connection with Edwin Waugh. Continue for another 250 yards along the narrow footpath and Waugh's Well is on the left. I hope you agree it was worth the effort!

Retrace your steps to the three-way junction of the concrete track, the track to the right of the wall and the one going up the hill to the right. Take the middle one, keeping the wall on your left. Go straight on, in the same direction, first track, then path, until you're back at the wooden signpost.

We're going to return to Rawtenstall from here by the same route but before we do, let's have a look at Marshall's 'surprise view' of the Rossendale Valley. At the signpost, go straight on, following the 'Pendle Bridleway to Waterfoot' sign. Within 200 yards, we have a very different view of the Rossendale Valley!

As an aide-memoire, I'll list the main points of the return route. Return to the signpost, turn right and take the track with Cowpe Lowe on your right and the wall on your left. At the deep ditch, turn left and follow the track downhill. Go over the stile into the field and descend, keeping the deep gulley on your left. At the bottom, join the track (Sand Beds Lane) and continue down the hill until you reach the junction with Gincroft Lane. Turn sharp right into Gincroft Lane, pass the gates, house and quarry on your right, then after a farm lane joins from the left, go straight on, pass through the farmyard and exit onto the long, straight, flat road.

Where the road bends to the left, after 30 yards take the path into the wood on the right. Descend through the wood to Lomas Lane, then follow it to Bury Road and turn right. Rawtenstall Railway Station is a little further on, on the left.

A morning's musings on Musbury Tor

I enjoy musing. I particularly enjoy musing on a hilltop. I can't remember the last time I heard that word being used in everyday conversation but contemplation, reflection, considering life's big picture is undoubtedly good for us. The best place to do so is, of course, on a Rossendale hilltop. Our most distinctive one is Musbury Tor and whilst thousands of people pass it in their cars on the M66 daily and probably think, "that's an unusual shape, I wonder how you get there?", very few make the effort. It's a short walk with a spectacular view from the top on a clear day.

Before we do that, let's read Marshall's musings. Again, this is a much-shortened version as he mused at considerable length.

Marshall says: *"I shall never forget the first impressions made upon my mind by the hills of Rossendale. A life previously spent in crowded cities, where the only altitudes upon which the eye could rest* *were the steeples of churches and the chimneys of manufactories, made mountain scenery a startling change to me. It is true I was somewhat familiar with their outline; but a man must live amongst them ere he understands them or is fully impressed with their majesty and strength. When first I made my home beneath their shadow, I was seized with an indescribable fear lest they should shelve down and they seemed to have a far-off look, which led me to suppose the scaling of their summits herculean toil. At last I ventured to climb the tops of the nearest range when, instead of looking out upon an extending plain, or a precipitate descent, as anticipated, to my astonishment I found ridge after ridge of heathery wilderness, and billowy moorlands of furze and fern and cotton grass. The surprise at this sight well-nigh overcame me; fear from a sense of loneliness and awe from a sense of the illimitable seized me.*

One of our stateliest, though by no means one of our highest, hills is Musbury Tor. No traveller can pass through the valley without being struck with its graceful slopes and prominent form. Starting from the banks of the Irwell, its slope rises gently towards Sunnybank and Musbury Farm and then, suddenly stiffening, reaches its summit some 1,115 feet above the level of the sea. The top is circular and flat and the counter slope of the hill falls somewhat precipitately into the gorge that runs between Musbury and the range of hills forming the west flank of the Grane Valley.

I know of no finer view than the one presenting itself to the eye of the spectator as he stands upon the summit of this Tor. He is engirdled by the hills; on every side they lift themselves in silent majesty, robed in never-fading green. Here and there the outlines are somewhat broken and heaps of shale tell from whence their treasures have been torn; while quietly sleeping beneath the shadow of their tops a hundred farmsteads lie. Nearer to the great highways which men have ploughed out of their sides for the transit of merchandise, the mansions of the wealthy stand and by the banks of streams the mills which make our valley famous for its cotton goods rise in their many storeys and point their grimy chimneys to the sky. River and rail, running for miles together, record a tale of competition and industry, and the scattered towers and spires of churches remind one of the rest that remaineth on the first day of the week for the busy workers who people this far outreaching scene of rural and manufacturing life.

By way of direction, reach Helmshore Station either by road or rail, turn down what is known as Station Brow, keep along Station Road until the old, seven-storied, disused mill is reached, follow the road running up by its side until you gain the foot of the Tor, and then you may make your choice of a half-dozen pathways, all of which lead to its summit.

When I at last scaled the crest, I threw myself down upon a ledge of rock warmed by the sun, and, closing my eyes, gave myself up to those strange and fitful sounds only heard among the hills. As I did so, there came stealing upward the playful voice of children, gathering winberries among the bushes far below my feet, the shrill treble of a woman's voice in some distant farmstead calling to her bairns or to her poultry, the monotonous barking of a dog, perchance scaring away some tramp, the whirl of the train as it rushed down the Helmshore cutting bearing its living freight to the city below, the never-ceasing rustle of the ferns and grasses as they were swept by the ever-moaning wind. These mingled sounds all came borne in upon me and touched me with a soothing spell.

In a little while I arose and looked down upon Musbury, or the hill of moss, and my thoughts wandered back to the time when it was the Park, or Laund, of the Forest of Rossendale maintained for fattening the larger animals for the table of the king and nobles. I thought, too, of the hunts that had taken place upon its slopes, of the swift-footed hound coursing its pasturage after prey, of the stag at bay in its fastnesses, and of the merry laugh of lord and liegeman that must oftentimes have responded to the hunts-man's horn. And then my musing took another backward leap and I thought of the legions of Imperial Rome as they marched along the famous road known as Watling Street, which ran by the western side of the hill whereon I stood, and of beacon fires lighted upon its summits, and weary watchings from its coigns of vantage in the days when the surrounding stretches of land were morasses, and the encircling hills were clothed with trees."

Can we follow his route? Yes

Walk 8: Circular walk from Snig Hole Park to Musbury Tor

Distance: 2 miles

Features: lovely views of the Musbury Valley as we climb the Tor and over much of Manchester and beyond, once there.

Terrain: from the bottom of the Tor, it is a continuous climb, sometimes steep; gates and stiles (some very high); very uneven underfoot in places; can be muddy.

Starting point: the entrance to Snig Hole Park on Helmshore Road (B6214), Helmshore. Near-ish postcode BB4 4LQ.

Parking / Public transport: There is no parking in Snig Hole Park so park on-street nearby. Helmshore is about half a mile away and served by buses.

Route: From Snig Hole Park entrance with its three stone pillars, walk 100 yards up Helmshore Road to the replica 'signal box' house. This is the former site of Helmshore Railway Station. A short section of the old railway cutting can be seen to the right but housing has obliterated the line of the railway to the left. Return to the start point and turn right into Station Road. Follow the road over the River Ogden, first on your left and then your right. When it meets Holcombe Road, bear right. After passing the converted mill buildings on your left, turn left into Park Road and take the walled, stone track straight ahead (signed 'Musbury Road' on an old mill stone) up the hill.

After a quarter of a mile, pass to the left of the farmhouse and continue, keeping a wall on your left. In the next field, go to the right of the trees and gulley and walk up the hill parallel to them. Pass through a gate between two intersecting walls and go straight on, up the hill, keeping the wall on your right. In one hundred yards, take the grass path on the left, in the 7 o'clock direction (almost back on yourself), to continue your climb to the top.

The path climbs around the edge of the Tor and, after a fence joins on the left near the top, bends to the right between two piles of stone and shale. From here, you can explore the plateau but, before doing so, make a mental note of where the path ends, as you need to return to it to descend and the disused quarry workings can be disorienting.

It's not a pretty sight on top, the concept of restoration hadn't been invented and the quarry owners didn't clear up their mess when they left! Nevertheless, you're only yards away from the highest point and the view makes it all worthwhile. Find a vantage point, sit on a rock and muse.

Return to the path you came up, follow it to the left, down the hill. At a point before it takes a sharper bend to the left and with an impressive rock on the hill above you, take the path to the right at 4 o'clock, down to a wall with a stile. Cross the stile and head for the bottom left corner of the field. Cross the high stile into the next field and turn right, continuing downhill with the wall on your right.

Join a farm track next to a farm (Tor End Farm) and continue down the lane, passing through the next farmyard (right, left and right) and down the lane (Tor End Road) until it meets Holcombe Road. Turn right onto the road, then left after 20 yards, down a cobbled alley between two houses. Turn left at the bottom, opposite Alden Brook Apartments, and left at the junction with the main road. Your starting point is 30 yards on the right.

A ramble through Ravenshore on an Autumn afternoon

Marshall says: *"I plan my walks according to the season of the year. In mid-Winter I love to wander beneath the leafless trees and look at their delicate tracery of branches standing out in clear relief from the cold, blue sky beyond. In the Springtime, give me the hills, across whose tops the March wind sweeps: let me battle with it until every drop of blood tingles and my whole body is aglow. In Summer, commend me to the meadows, where flowers bloom and the long grasses wave in shadows, where the mower whets his scythe and children sport among the new-mown hay. But in the Fall I prefer the cloughs. I love the silence that reigns in them, the mists that enfold them, the many-coloured leaves, all aglow with autumnal tints, that strew their winding paths and lie*

burnished beneath their clear and tortuous streams. So as it was sere October, I passed through the iron gate to Snig Hole, and then on to the Ravenshore Clough.

Entering by the iron gate at Bridge End, I walked along the road dividing the hedge-bank, studded with age-worn alders and fence of thorns, from the slope of green, once the bed of an old mill lodge and now carpeted with verdure, beyond which flows the river, with its richly-sycamored shores. A hundred yards brought me to the ruins of an old mill, below which lies the fold of Snig Hole. Approaching this fold, the vista of the clough opens, black, columnar trunks standing out from the sward, and background of foliage, a winding pathway of flags losing itself amid their clusters and leading from the footbridge to the heights beyond.

Forsaking the bridge, and going through the fold, I climbed the wall, and found myself to the left of the river, which runs some twenty feet below, and pours itself in thunderous volume over a circular weir upon the lower level of its rocky beds. From this point the gorge rapidly deepens, the sides becoming steeper and the growth of trees more plentiful. Above are overhanging rocks, their surface a wealth of dying verdure while on the further side of the stream the long grasses and rushes lie beaten down and browned. Beyond, and seen through the thinning foliage, a ruined bridge spans the stream and links the roadway with a dis-used mill.

Upon a mere neck of pathway, I stay my steps, to take in the scene and muse thereon. Here were the ruins of Nature, and amidst them the ruins of the works of man. In the one I saw a despoiled year, the wreckage of the seasons; in the other, a despoiled structure, the wreckage wrought by manufacture's mighty advance and innovation. But there was this difference, the ruins of Nature prophesied renewal; those of man would only speed on to more rapid decay.

As I stood I thought of the multitudes who had toiled within those walls, rung up at early morn by the clanging bell and hurrying home with joyous heart when freed from labour at the close of day, their hands now as idle in the grave as the rusting shafting in the mill. I crossed the arch leading up to the yard and passing through the broken gates looked around the silent storeys and through pane-less window frames. I stepped down into the firehole, where a handful of ashes lay, and then passed into the engine-house where only the huge stone beds remained. Reascending and traversing the yard, I came upon an old water-wheel in rusty ruin, with mouldering lichens and grey mosses clinging to its rotting spokes.

From the mill there runs a level stretch of cinder-path, over-arched by trees and leading to the viaduct forever memorable on account of its proximity to the frightful Helmshore railway accident. This accident occurred in the days before the block system and catch-points were invented. Three heavily-laden trip-trains from Belle Vue were slowly climbing this, the heaviest gradient on the Lancashire and Yorkshire' Railway Company's service, when the coupling chains of the second train parted and caused the greater part of the carriages to reverse their motion and dash, with death-dealing speed, into the rear train. Many were killed, and many more were wounded; and in the now roofless houses scattered around this clough the dying and the dead were laid.

Lower down the clough the bed of the stream is sure to attract the eye of the observant traveller. There is nothing like it in our district; and gentlemen to whom I have shown it tell me that seldom in their travels have they seen anything comparable to it. It is of solid rock, twisted and scooped into a thousand fantastic forms; basined, channelled, under-mined, rippled into wavelets, seamed with mighty fissures, polished into smoothness and torn into jagged edge. Reader, if you have not seen it, see it by all means; and if you have seen it, see it again, and I think you will find out what Ruskin means by "rocks in agony" and" rocks in repose."

Emerging from the clough, I climbed the field-path towards the Cockham Farms. I first arrived at the lower Cockham, standing upon the brow of the hill, and facing south. Following the cart ruts between the holly bushes on one side and a little clough on the other, I came to the Middle Cockham Farm. At one time it was fronted by an imposing porch, where food and clothing were dispensed to the poor at the midsummer and Christmas of each year. This charity was long since transferred to the Parish Church of Haslingden, where it is yet distributed at Christmastide.

A chill wind swept across the fields, a harbinger of the closing year, and bearing along upon its invisible current the seared and fallen leaves. A mist arose from the depths of the clough and slowly swept the meadows, giving exaggerated proportions to the farms and warning me that it was dangerous to loiter. Heeding the warning, I passed the Old Out Barn and Hall to Ewood Station, thankful that amid the stern realities and commercial strain of Rossendale, there were still seasons for quiet and scenes where fancy could wander free."

Can we follow his route? Yes, although at the end of the gorge where Marshall heads east to catch his train home, we visit Irwell Vale village and return on a parallel path above the gorge.

Walk 9: Circular walk from Snig Hole Park to Irwell Vale through Ravenshore Gorge

Distance: 2 miles

Features: a Victorian railway station and a gorgeous gorge.

Terrain: some gradients, one quite steep; stiles and gates; some very uneven ground; sometimes very muddy through the gorge.

Starting point: the entrance to Snig Hole Park on Helmshore Road (B6214), Helmshore. Near-ish postcode BB4 4LQ.

Parking / Public transport: there is no parking in Snig Hole Park, so park on-street nearby. Helmshore is about half a mile away and is served by buses.

Route: Enter the Park through the three stone pillars and follow the broad track with the children's play area to your right. Continue to the row of cottages by the river. This is Snig Hole. Take the path to the left, so that the cottages are on your left and the river on your right.

Follow this path, keeping the river on your right, through the gorge. The photograph on the front cover was taken beyond the viaduct and from the other direction.

When you emerge into a field, the grass path divides. Take the left fork and follow the path across the field to a gate, then turn right onto the road. Cross the road bridge over the River Ogden and immediately turn left. Cross the white-painted bridge and at the mini-roundabout bear right and then left into Hardsough Lane to visit Irwell Vale Railway

Station. If the steam trains are running, it's a very special place to see one. If not, it's delightful anyway!

Retrace your steps over the white-painted bridge and then, at the next bridge, turn left into Bowker Street. At the end of the street, bear right into Milne Street, which soon becomes a rough track and climbs out of the village.

At the top, after it bends to the left, go over the bridge, then stay on the track which bends to the right. At a Y shaped junction at the brow of the hill, take the right fork. At the next junction where a track drops to the right to a house, go straight on, on the main track. Cross the river at Snig Hole and where the track merges with another, bear left and follow it back to the Park entrance.

Grane Head

It's interesting how perceptions change. Marshall's opening sentence describes the Grane Valley as wild and bleak yet, today, it's as close to 'chocolate box picturesque' as we get in Rossendale with reservoirs, woodlands, streams and, if you can spot them, deer. Our route takes us through an old stone quarry which he disliked and which today, though not pretty, has a certain 'post-industrial' charm. In fact, if it was a slate quarry and in North Wales, it would be a tourist attraction. The boggart that he mentions, was the term used for pixies, elves and poltergeist activity.

Marshall says: *"The valley of the Grane is a wild, bleak, outlying district, bounded on the south-east by Musbury Heights and on the south-west by Haslingden Moor. It starts at Holden Wood, and, after running up for a distance of four miles, merges into the hills beyond, there being no outlet, save by scaling* *the tops, or following the steep tread of the old turnpike road to the busy towns of Blackburn and Darwen. The bed of this valley was once a rich flat of pasturage, through which the Ogden ran; but it has long since been dammed up by the Corporation of Bury and used as a storage ground for their water. The heights on either side, once thickly planted with trees, are now almost swept of vegetation; though there are old inhabitants still living who remember many a Summer's evening spent beneath their foliage and many a feast from their fallen nuts. The old life, too, is fast departing. Here and there we meet with one whose hoary hairs link him with the past, and who, with garrulous tongue, will talk of days for ever gone.*

He will tell us of times gone by when "Grane folk got their warps from Haslingden and carried back their pieces on their backs", when they "brewed" their whisky "up th' nook," or "deawn 'ith hoil;" and then, perchance, drawing his hand across his mouth, and smacking his lips, he will remark, in semi-soliloquy, "an' it war gradely stuff an' o'." He can paint for us the Grane as he knew it in his childhood, when "there were nowt but wood" and tell of summer droughts and winter snows which the children of this generation have never known. He remembers "bein' ta'en by his faither to see the bull baited at th' Howden Arms" and he'd "yeard his mother speak many a time of th' boggart deawn in cloof." He's seen many a "feight," and many an eating "doment." And then, in a far-off, sorrowful tone, he tells us, "There were noan so mony of th' owd folk left nea: those were gradely times, those were."

Passing into the valley, we notice an old and many-gabled building on the opposite side of the road to the Holden Arms. This is Holden Hall, the building, together with its estate, passing into the hands of Henry Maden, Esq., J.P. of Bacup. Henry lived during the reign of Edward IV., and married Margery, daughter of Thomas Harrington. The Harrington's were engaged in the civil wars then raging and after a disastrous defeat in which Margery had father and brother slain, another brother, who escaped, fled to Holden Hall for safety beneath his sister's roof. But here he found none, for her husband was the sworn foe of the defeated party. Hence Madge was compelled to hide her brother in a cave over which the Holden Reservoir now stretches its placid sheet of waters, and where, from time to time, she visited him and ministered to his wants. These visits, which were frequent and clandestine, roused the jealousy of her husband, who, suspecting her fidelity, watched her, witnessed the meeting, and mistaking the brother for the paramour, drew his sword, and delivered the fatal blow. But it smote the one for whom it was not intended, for Madge rushed in, and died in her brother's stead. To this day, the spot is known as "Madge Lamb", lamb being a cave or hole in a clough and the wraith of the beautiful Madge is still said to haunt the shadowy recesses of the glen.

Leaving Holden Hall and crossing the road embankment of the lower reservoir, we gain the farther side of the valley and for the next three miles traverse the Under Heights Plantation. These heights rise precipitately from the reservoir bank to a height of two hundred and fifty feet, their ridges scarped with quarries and their vegetation destroyed by heaps of shale shot over from the neighbouring delfs. To reach these heights we keep the path that runs along the upper bank of the reservoir, turning off at the stile in the wall of the third field, and leading to the ruins of Rake Foot Farm. Thence we take the foot road running under the hills and passing beneath the tram lines to Higher Scars.

From this point we cautiously hurry past the tips to Northampton, beyond which lies the Hog Lough Clough, and climb the opposite bank, gaining a field path which rounds the foot of a richly-pastured mound. In the ditch below us is a rare growth of wild flower. The golden censer of the Marshmarigold, the delicate veined snow-white petals of the Woodsorrel, the starlike fringe of the Stitchwort, and the dreamy blue of the waving Hyacinth of the woods, these are all woven in richest pattern into the breast of bank along which we pass.

Passing through the gate, we foot the bridge, and drop down into the bed of the stream whose source we purpose to explore. At first we trip lightly from boulder to boulder, huge stones rounded and polished by the plash and play of many waters, next to find ourselves upon shelving lengths of rock, over which the stream smoothly lips and shimmers in the light of summer skies. Soon the banks on either side become steeper, and gloomily close in, until at last, towards the head, they rise some thirty feet, and encircle us with a rounded sweep of overhanging rock.

This, however, is but the first and lower of the cloughs, the holy place, not the holy of holies. Another ascent ere this is reached. So we retrace our steps until able to climb the bank to the heights beyond. This done, we find and follow the course of this upper stream. Here the rocky walls are wilder and barren of all growth, and the bed of the stream is narrower and less easy of ascent. At last, we front a fall of waters, not precipitate, but shelving, in low, long steps. With gentle tread we ascend this mossy stairway of the naiads and once upon its landing, stand within their home. Here dwells, amid the silence of its music, and the solitude of its companionship, the Spirit of the Stream.

On our return, we resolved to interview Andrew Scholes, the well-known hermit of the Grane. No difficulty was experienced in finding his home; the difficulty was in securing an interview with the man, for the moment he saw us he beat a hasty retreat and barred his door. Left thus in the cold, we conversed with a man who was assisting him with his hay, and who informed us, among other things, that he and his brother were the only men in the Grane who could dance the "March of the Duke of York." This, he said, was no mean accomplishment. But as we had set out to see Andrew, we were disloyal enough to be indifferent to the Duke of York. We pressed him to bring about an interview, but the question was, how much? At last a few coppers won him over and he entered the house, soon to return and bid us follow.

We entered and beheld upon the threshold the remains of what once had been a man. A tall, round-shouldered, hairy-visaged monster, with twinkling eye and leering look, half-scared, half-savage, with face all seamed with lines of dirt and age. A three-legged table, bearing an earthen pot and spoon, stood in the middle of the windowless room, the spaces between the jambs being built up with stones. Against the wall a cart without wheels was reared on its side, which Andrew in his spare hours had constructed within his dwelling, and for which he found no use. He asked us what we wanted, and we told him we had heard he possessed a violin of value, and begged that we might hear him touch its "trembling strings" but it was only when we backed our request by a fee of sixpence that he brought out "the merry bit timber." Settling himself down upon the remains of a chair, he drew the bow across the strings and sung some moorland ditty, now beyond recall. My friend, a violinist, then took up the instrument and scraped out "the Last Rose of Summer" in such wailing notes that I fled into the open again, and entered into conversation with the man whose toes could keep time to "The glorious Duke of York." He told me that Andrew came of a fairly good family and that from his youth he had been of seclusive habits, and over some trifling dispute left his home and friends, to follow a solitary moorland life. Alone he had lived for fifty years and alone he supposed he would die. Then, calling attention to a carved slab, on which were inscribed some lines of poetry, he said, "Andrew made those up out of his own 'ead, and cut them on that stone." I read them, and thus they run:

"Happy the man, the only happy man, that out of choice doth all the good he can. Who business leaves, and others better makes by the prudent industry and the pains he takes. While he lives he's man's esteem, and when he dies his fame will follow him."

As we turned to leave this hermitage, there opened upon us one of those sweeps of landscape for which Rossendale and its surrounding districts are famous. The valley lay outstretched in mighty undulation, all robed in glorious green. In the bottom lands the cattle browsed, the farmsteads dotting the hills, and the moors crowning the tops. Far away, the winding roads ran in circuitous trend, losing themselves as they dipped over distant ridges. The placid sheets of storage water shimmered in the sunlight and stretched the valley's length. Old mills, some in ruins and some running, abutted upon the friendly streams, and puffs of steam told where the tramcars from the quarries wound their way. The hamlet of Grane lay snug and peaceful, old houses telling of its antiquity, and the spire of its church bespeaking the presence of God. So we homewards found our way, pausing now and then to chat with folks that sunned themselves by cottage doors, and lingering long at Phineas Fold and Crow Trees, the two chief monuments of the former domestic glory of the Grane."

Can we follow his route? Yes but only as far as Grane Head, not to the source of the River Ogden.

Walk 10: Figure of eight walk from Haslingden Cemetery to Grane Head

Distance: 5 miles

Features: an impressive disused stone quarry, woodland, lovely views of the Grane Valley.

Terrain: some steep gradients; stiles and gates; very uneven ground; can be very muddy.

Starting point: Haslingden Cemetery gates / Holden Arms pub / Holden Wood Antiques Centre. Near-ish postcode BB4 4PD.

Parking / Public transport: park on-street nearby. There is a bus service along Grane Road.

Route: Marshall says that he could see Holden Hall from his starting point. It was located on the hillside behind the cemetery but has since been demolished.

From the road junction, walk along Holcombe Road and, almost immediately, take the lane to right of the first house on the right. After it dips, with the reservoir on the right and the outlet on the left, it takes a sharp bend to the right. Go through the pedestrian gate to the left of a full-width gate.

Pass two gated farm roads on your left. After the second one the lane becomes a track and after a further 100 yards, take the footpath on your left, through a metal kissing gate into a field. Walk in a 1 o'clock direction up the field and, in the top right-hand corner, cross a stile. Walk across a small field in a 2 o'clock direction and cross two stiles next to each other. After another 15 yards, the path divides. Take the right fork onto a paved, field path.

An impressive stone wall appears in front of you and the path bends to the right in front of it. The wall is, in fact, the remains of a tramway incline used to take stone from the quarry above to the valley below. Cut through the tunnel on your left or follow the path around the incline to continue along it as it runs roughly parallel to the reservoir.

Where a path joins from the left, bear right over a stream and continue, passing a ruined cottage on your right and, eventually, a large, solitary (and beautifully shaped) tree, also on your right.

This is 'Northampton', yes, really! Continue with a ditch on your left and then cross a wooden bridge and stay on the path with woods ahead and to your left. Cross another footbridge (over Hog Lowe Clough), then take the steps immediately on your left towards the wood. Continue on the path for a quarter of a mile to another footbridge.

This is Ogden Brook and is as close as we can get to the river's source. Marshall walked up the stream-bed from here to find it! A little up-stream is the area known as Grane Head.

Cross the footbridge, go up the steps to the left and follow the path through the woods, passing two stone gate-posts on your left.

After 250 yards, go down the steps to join the main path that runs around the reservoir. Turn left, over a bridge, and follow the broad path up the hill, then along the top with the woods on your left. The remains of cottages and the information boards are interesting. Descend to the trees in front of you, then take the path to the right and cross the reservoir dam.

Having crossed the outlet bridge, turn left into a field and walk up the hill to the solitary tree. Turn left onto the path just above it.

Pass the remains of the cottage, now on your left and, a little further on, where the path crosses a stream and then divides, take the right fork up the hill.

Continue on this path. It eventually curves to the right, crosses the remains of a wall and then bends to the left through a gap in another wall. Within a few yards, a path goes straight on but ours bends to the right between two earth mounds and emerges onto a plateau with the remains of buildings, piles of stone and a tall chimney.

Make your way to the chimney and bear left in front of it, so that the building remains are on your left and the chimney on your right.

This is the start of a broad track. Go straight on, ignoring tracks off to the right, and descend for about half a mile. One hundred yards after a farm track joins from the left, as the lane begins to bend to the right, turn left, through a metal gate on a grassy bank, onto a footpath.

The footpath emerges next to a house on your right. Follow the lane down the hill, pass another house also on your right and descend through a field, keeping a wall on your left. The lane takes a sharp left turn and a gentle right bend to a full-width gate with a stile to its right. Cross the stile, turn right onto the lane and follow it back to the starting point.

…. and finally

In this book I have only scratched the surface of the wonderful legacy that Marshall Mather has left us and I continue my journey of discovery in 'More Victorian Rossendale Walks' and 'Victorian Rossendale Walks: The End of an Era'. I hope you enjoy these rambles as much as Marshall did and I do.

Have fun out there and stay safe!

Andrew Gill: I have collected early photographs and optical antiques for over forty years. I am a professional 'magic lantern' showman presenting lantern slide shows and giving talks on Victorian optical entertainments for museums, festivals, special interest groups and universities. For information about magic lanterns and slides and to contact me, please visit my website **Magic Lantern World** at www.magiclanternist.com

I have published historical booklets and photo albums on the subjects below. They are available from amazon, some as printed books, some as e-books, many in both formats. To see them all and 'look inside', simply search for one of my titles, then click the 'Andrew Gill' link. Alternatively, go to the 'My photo-history booklets' page on my website (see above) and click on the link.

Historical travel guides
Jersey in 1921
Norwich in 1880
Doon the Watter
Liverpool in 1886
Nottingham in 1899
Bournemouth in 1914
Great Yarmouth in 1880
Victorian Walks in Surrey
The Way We Were: Bath
A Victorian Visit to Brighton
A Victorian Visit to Hastings
A Victorian Visit to Falmouth
Newcastle upon Tyne in 1903
Victorian and Edwardian York
The Way We Were: Llandudno
Doncaster: The Way We Were
Victorian and Edwardian Leeds
The Way We Were: Manchester
Victorian and Edwardian Bradford
Victorian and Edwardian Sheffield
A Victorian Visit to Fowey and Looe
A Victorian Visit to Peel, Isle of Man
The Way We Were: The Lake District
Lechlade to Oxford by Canoe in 1875
Guernsey, Sark and Alderney in 1921
East Devon through the Magic Lantern
The River Thames from Source to Sea
North Devon through the Magic Lantern
A Victorian Visit to Ramsey, Isle of Man
A Victorian Visit to Douglas, Isle of Man
Victorian Totnes through the Magic Lantern

Victorian Whitby through the Magic Lantern
Victorian London through the Magic Lantern
St. Ives through the Victorian Magic Lantern
Victorian Torquay through the Magic Lantern
Victorian Glasgow through the Magic Lantern
The Way We Were: Wakefield and Dewsbury
The Way We Were: Hebden Bridge to Halifax
Victorian Edinburgh through the Magic Lantern
Victorian Scarborough through the Magic Lantern
The Way We Were: Hull and the surrounding area
The Way We Were: Harrogate and Knaresborough
A Victorian Tour of North Wales: Rhyl to Llandudno
A Victorian Visit to Lewes and the surrounding area
The Isle of Man through the Victorian Magic Lantern
A Victorian Visit to Helston and the Lizard Peninsula
A Victorian Railway Journey from Plymouth to Padstow
A Victorian Visit to Barmouth and the Surrounding Area
A Victorian Visit to Malton, Pickering and Castle Howard
A Victorian Visit to Eastbourne and the surrounding area
A Victorian Visit to Aberystwyth and the Surrounding Area
A Victorian Visit to Castletown, Port St. Mary and Port Erin
Penzance and Newlyn through the Victorian Magic Lantern
A Victorian Journey to Snowdonia, Caernarfon and Pwllheli
Victorian Brixham and Dartmouth through the Magic Lantern
Victorian Plymouth and Devonport through the Magic Lantern
A Victorian Tour of North Wales: Conwy to Caernarfon via Anglesey
Staithes, Runswick and Robin Hood's Bay through the Magic Lantern
A Victorian Visit to Cornwall: Morwenstow to Tintagel via Kilkhampton, Bude, Boscastle and Bossiney
Dawlish, Teignmouth and Newton Abbot through the Victorian Magic Lantern

Other historical topics
Sarah Jane's Victorian Tour of Scotland
The River Tyne through the Magic Lantern
The 1907 Wrench Cinematograph Catalogue
Victorian Street Life through the Magic Lantern
The First World War through the Magic Lantern
Ballyclare May Fair through the Victorian Magic Lantern
The Story of Burnley's Trams through the Magic Lantern
The Franco-British 'White City' London Exhibition of 1908
The 1907 Wrench 'Optical and Science Lanterns' Catalogue
How They Built the Forth Railway Bridge: A Victorian Magic Lantern Show

Walking Books
Victorian Rossendale Walks
More Victorian Rossendale Walks
Victorian Walks on the Isle of Wight (Book 1)
Victorian Walks on the Isle of Wight (Book 2)
Victorian Rossendale Walks: The End of an Era

Historical photo albums (just photos)
The Way We Were: Suffolk
Norwich: The Way We Were
Sheffield: The Way We Were

The Way We Were: Somerset
Fife through the Magic Lantern
York through the Magic Lantern
Rossendale: The Way We Were
The Way We Were: Lincolnshire
The Way We Were: Cumberland
Burnley through the Magic Lantern
Oban to the Hebrides and St. Kilda
Tasmania through the Magic Lantern
New York through the Magic Lantern
Swaledale through the Magic Lantern
Llandudno through the Magic Lantern
Birmingham through the Magic Lantern
Penzance, Newlyn and the Isles of Scilly
Great Yarmouth through the Magic Lantern
Ancient Baalbec through the Magic Lantern
The Isle of Skye through the Magic Lantern
Ancient Palmyra through the Magic Lantern
The Kentish Coast from Whitstable to Hythe
New South Wales through the Magic Lantern
From Glasgow to Rothesay by paddle steamer
Victorian Childhood through the Magic Lantern
The Way We Were: Yorkshire Railway Stations
Southampton, Portsmouth and the Great Liners
Newcastle upon Tyne through the Magic Lantern
Egypt's Ancient Monuments through the Magic Lantern
The Way We Were: Birkenhead, Port Sunlight and the Wirral
Ancient Egypt, Baalbec and Palmyra through the Magic Lantern

Birmingham through the Magic Lantern
Bournemouth in 1914
A travel guide and photographs from one hundred years ago
A Victorian Visit to Brighton
A Victorian Tour of North Wales: Conwy to Caernarfon via Anglesey
Ballyclare May Fa
through the Victor
Magic Lantern
Dawlish, Teignmouth and Newton Abbot through the Victorian Magic Lantern
Photographs from magic lantern slides and text from a Victorian travel guide
Fife through the Magic Lantern
The Way We Were
Cumberland
Great Yarmouth through the Magic Lantern
A Victorian Visit to Peel, Isle of Man
Oban to the Hebride and St. Kilda
The Kentish Coast from Whitstable to Hythe
Victorian Walks on the Isle of Wight
Victorian Plymouth and Devonport through the Magic Lantern
Thirty five 'magic lantern' photos and text from an 1883 travel guide
Staithes, Runswick and Robin Hood's Bay through the Magic Lantern
Victorian Street Life through the Magic Lantern
The River Thames from Source to Sea
How They Built the Forth Railway Bridge
Southampton, Portsmouth and the Great Liners
CLOTHING

Printed in Poland
by Amazon Fulfillment
Poland Sp. z o.o., Wrocław